C000130209

MOON MILK

Rachel Bower was born in Bradford, 1980, and now lives in Sheffield. She is a Leverhulme Research Fellow at the University of Leeds, and is the founder of Verse Matters, a feminist arts collective in Sheffield. She is the author of *Epistolarity and World Literature, 1980-2010* (Palgrave Macmillan, 2017) and editor of *Verse Matters* (with Helen Mort; Valley Press, 2017). Find her on Twitter @rachelebower.

Moon Milk

RACHEL BOWER

Valley Press

First published in 2018 by Valley Press
Woodend, The Crescent, Scarborough, YO11 2PW
www.valleypressuk.com

First edition, first printing (June 2018)

ISBN 978-1-908853-83-7
Cat. no. VP0118

A CIP record for this book is available from the British Library.

Cover and text design by Jamie McGarry.

Printed and bound in the EU by Pulsio, Paris.

Supported using public funding by
ARTS COUNCIL
ENGLAND
LOTTERY FUNDED

Contents

for Jude, Esme, Otto and the ones lost in-between

and for Jake, my anchor

One Line

again.
I hold it by the window
then under a lamp
almost touching
the bulb
to force
that second stripe
to appear,
squinting
to get one up
on this monthly trickery
of blankness.

This is not
the bright bone
of holly
or the crunch
of frost
or even a gulp
of milk
from the fridge,
but just another
moonless belly
and waiting
again.

Two Lines

of pink
lemonade
fizz
on a strip
in my pocket.
Bubbles
tickle
my fingers
every time
I check
and my neck
flushes
as I leave
the Arndale
toilets.

I am frizzante
blush
and excitement
and a petal
of fear.
Raspberries
dance
secret
tracks
on the stick
and a dot
glows
a bit
brighter
in my womb.

Speck

I did not see a dot of gold
dancing in the crimson steam
but I knew you were there

pumped with engine spores
and fog from a puffball,
iron clouds from that factory

always packed to the rafters
with starlings. I asked them politely
to *stop the cogs!* and *turn the turbine off!*

so I could look for you properly
but they only trilled gloss green
and metal wings.

They said *there's only clots and old bolts*
but I knew you were there,
a speckle in the swirl

of brittlegill and rust
pumped by sparrow pistons
as the axle rattled on.

Soul Seed

I could not know that the flood of after-birth
and early-birth and missed-birth, does not only flow
bright and clean but also falls as offal.

That a blood clot is not a tight cluster of stars
but the wet shine of kidney, of spleen, of maws.
I squatted, calves flecked with liver, wiped the spoiled floor.

The sonographer would not let me see the screen
as she searched for your soul and found only scree
and lumps of congealed sun

black as sackcloth made of hair.
A tattered inkhorn with upturned belly,
a seed burnished to lead.

When the blood and iodine on my thighs
hardened to a slab of brittle rhubarb candy,
I cracked it carefully with a silver toffee hammer

and when the silence of my friends
began to wrap my face,
I popped a piece in and sucked.

Cherries

Sometimes habits pull you through
and you wonder if it should be scuffed
and slack and holding hands
in the dark, bristle calved, taking
turns to spit in the sink and piss.
Or if it should gleam tight like a cherry.

You wonder if this is the taste of bruises
from the bag, whether the crash of juice
in your ears will stop when the rot sets in,
whether it's better to shrivel as a pair
on the stalk or pluck now – *softest pop* –
and lick sweet sap from the wound.

Ultrasound

We did not come seeking bones
but the spark that makes bones flicker –
the wrinkle of pearl that says
this one is breathing

this one is gulping sweet liquor
this one has fishbones finer than seconds –
needle ribs, feathers caught in a wave
this one is breathing

liquid breath, it bubbles to his core
and fills his snowball belly

this one is breathing.

Hope

We call them lines of desire:
bald patches of grass, blades of glass
soil packed and buffed to a sheen.

Our fingers glow with white rings:
ridges of wax, rubbed metal on bone
thin bands of crystal glaze.

The land shines with ginger again.

Fruit

That July there were no sweet yellow mangoes from Pakistan
(they said this would stop insects at the border).
I chewed candied lemon instead and quenched my ankles in buckets of ice.

I belonged only to you in those sweltering days, belly to belly
blood to blood. The fumes were loud but the window stayed open all night.
Even my organs made way for you. My heart galloped for us both.

My ribcage expanded, packed with wriggling birds.
Stray feathers even poked from my naval! You kicked everything,
inside and out, a raspberry rash spread round my middle.

My feet became paddle fruit, slapping the pavements while my fingers swelled
to bananas. Melon faced, I sat in and sucked nectarines.
Sometimes the birds pecked but they rarely slept.

The ancient grocer predicted a girl, then a boy. She told me about the fire
she'd fled in Karachi when she was big with her first.
That doused the heat of my inner-city street.

She slipped me satsumas and pears when she could. She wrapped her white dupatta
close round her face and whispered about cloves and brothers,
star-fruit and mothers. Strangers patted my belly, told me it was only water

but I knew you weren't liquid. You were my little dragon fruit
practicing flames and flight in the middle of the night
and resting, by light, on the warm plum floor of our cave.

Slow Ship

32 weeks

We are a slow ship now, hefty and flat,
but mighty on waves that rock the yachts
and trawlers that flit around us.

Quicksilvers spin tightly round corners
breezing past our bulk, as we turn, awkward,
making barely perceptible progress towards the land.

I have heard hearts gallop
and suspect they power this ferry,
harnessed to timber and cogs

pounding circles, day and night.
It's supposed to be steam now
not paddles and wheels

but we know secret charts
plotted quietly with golden tools.
It's a reverse voyage really

unstoppering the mouths of our dead,
removing the coins that
Hades placed in their mouths,

payment for the journey.
I keep these safely in my sea chest
and prepare to split our souls

as ancestors spill over railings
bright hair floating around our keel
spirits gleaming in shoals of fish.

They silver the tar of our hull
tracing the route to buttery shores,
to the sands where calves are born.

Arc

36 weeks, 5 days

You have made an orb of me,
  this flat pebble of midriff
    no longer good for skimming,
    swollen with bright becks,
    your story carved in rock.

    Ditches rise to cairns
   and I lean back and watch
    shelducks mining freckles,
   wondering at the breakers
that crest as you stretch and roll.

Waiting

I scrutinise my nipples for sap
but I'm not even sure where to look,
listen carefully for a splash
of colour but hear nothing I know.

It's been months of course
but I think you might not come now
and even with your head between my walking legs
I do not know where you are.

In time my body will prove wiser
and when all that raspberry tea and swirling
does not bring you any quicker
I feel into age-old maps of women.
You will come when it is time.

Aubade

I wake with you in a nest.
We are still one in the dark.

They kept the frankincense smoking all night
   but it didn't curl up here.

Everything is moss and bark.

I am smudged with muck and salt.
They say it will be a good day's plough.

Your heart has bloomed with mine
   for nine long months, but soon it will be time

for the wrench of dawn
to crack yolk on our basket of blood.

Each iron grip brings us closer
to becoming two my love   but I will always be yours.

Ostare is rising now
with her milk-flower butterfly frock.

They will flutter to us soon
and leave her naked   her body stripped to earth
like mine. And I know they will try to heal

the split cord

flitting from my nipple to your lips
    silver umbilicals   in the air.

They will stretch this glowing trail for us
for many dawns to come   to help me let go.

They will dust wings on blistered cheeks
    coat my forehead with eggshell frost.

But now the wings batter at our nest.

I blink and know it is time.

Stones

after Tomas Tranströmer

I keep trying to relax
                    but hear howling
from the bed next door
                    glass-clear as if there
were no curtain between us
as if this is the most
                    unnatural thing
in the world
and I listen to fear
                    and breathe again
my body is made for this
          and wish for alpine streams
                    to smooth our stones
for ancient women
          to trample moans
                    through sweet grass
and gift us maps of crags
                    trace the way
pebble paths to guide us
          through the strip-lights
                    of this place
to stroke our stainless sheets
          and when I hear
                    the crystal scream
legs in the air
          I wish her the darkest hush of pine.

Foaling

Nobody told me I would become a beast
during labour
four fingers open, a horse measured in hands.

I whinnied and brayed but no-one understood –
they tacked me up
anyway and let me shit on the floor.

When my legs buckled they walked round me,
tidied the stalls,
talked among themselves, indifferent to my cries.

They packed me into a truck
but I bolted,
thighs blazing as I charged through the stars.

I paused at last in a patch of black grass
sweet taste of blood
and, alone in the dark, birthed my foal.

Track

She tramps this path each year, head of trees held high
defending lime lichen and sweet tundra grass for belly swell.
She swallows quickly. Her milk will be rich when she's back.

They tread the track with her, thousands of wide hooves
heading north in steaming packs. To believe in the path
is to trust the stink of plum earth and her wet velvet.

She weaves her way back in spring, antlers dropping
just before her calf. The birth is silent. She rests and stands
as thin legs emerge. She licks him clean as he knew she would.

Postnatal Ward

after Natalie Diaz

I stand sobbing at the window in my pyjamas as
my Mum pulls into a layby to take the call.
There are wasps all over this place, I say
I can hear them buzzing, Mum.

My Mum pulls into a layby to take the call
What do you mean, wasps? Have you told anyone?
I can hear them buzzing, Mum.
They're in the offensive waste.

She asks *What do you mean, wasps? Are they real?*
The dinner trolley hums yellow and black outside the door.
They're in the offensive waste
Please come quickly. It's so hot in here.

The dinner trolley hums yellow and black outside the door.
There must be a nest, I say. *What if they land on his face.*
Please come quickly. It's so hot in here.
Mum winces. *I'm on my way.*

But there must be a nest, I say. *What if they land on his face.*
Can you hear them Mum?
Mum winces. *I'm on my way.*
The walls are clammy, the colour of porridge.

(cont.)

Can you hear them Mum?
Oh God, now they're going for his spine.
The walls are clammy, the colour of porridge.
Now the floor is starting to vibrate

Oh God, now they're going for his spine.
I stand sobbing at the window in my pyjamas as
the floor starts to vibrate
I hear it, she says, *I'm coming.*

New Beginnings

We are starting again
this wrinkly belly and me,

learning how to walk again,
even how to talk

to strangers without
the shield of peach cheeks.

We are tottering
through the retail park

off kilter but determined
to find a latte and drink it hot,

even if the milk soaks our shirt
even though we're waddling,

still bruised from birth.
I think of him safe,

scan the tarmac again
without anchor.

Our balance is off.
You shrivel in my hollow

as I try to unfurl.
Only eighteen minutes left

until we see his starfish hands.
We wobble together and smile.

Amber

She sat on the sofa and watched tears leak
as I told her *I am a milk machine –*
I can only offer this, everyone says
put him down, he cannot be hungry, my blood
turns the milk pink, I can offer nothing else.

She said *milk is what he needs, you are all*
he needs, you are growing a person
take him into your bed and do what you feel.

I am all he needs. I hauled myself taller then,
mouth remembering my great great
grandma, before shame, before clockwork babies
when sisters knew milk has raspberry threads
and aunties pressed cabbage on breasts

and even though she never came back
she left resin on the cushion and my milk shone gold
and we sat for weeks in her glow.

Oyster

As he sleeps, I spoon light from the jug
and sprinkle it over the floorboards.

I work quickly, never knowing when he will wake.

Sometimes I dance through the house
papering the walls with glass,
offering petals and droplets of wax.

I hope to remember the woman I was
before he was born, the sculptor of rain

but when his small cry balloons
I become the milk that surges in,
his face a pearl in my palms.

Sugar Beet

*"Jiggle, jiggle, jiggle, jiggle, tickle, tickle, tickle, tickle,
little sack of sugar I could eat you up" – Woody Guthrie*

Pretending to eat cake
I sit you on the table just to look in your eyes
rub my nose with your nose kiss your toes
sticky hands on my lips and chin and we are lost
in a cloud of sweet flour.
In a cloud of sweet flour
we are lost, sticky hands on my lips and chin and
kiss your toes, rub my nose with your nose
just to look in your eyes, I sit you on the table
pretending to eat cake.

Knot

In the washer I tie my arms in knots
twisting one around the other, binding
black acrylic. I wind them tightly
at the elbow until the clutch is hard.
It takes me weeks to get my fingers
under a seam, blistered against
stiffness, pressing panicked creases
and when I hang myself to dry
my elbows are still twisted, slack spills
at the shoulder, acrylic kinks at the wrist.

Shard

I am a switch of white birch
a bleached witch
the crackle of ice
a slice of bright

I am a switch of white birch
a splinter of steel
the flash of bone
a shriek of stone

I am a switch of white birch
a stripped spine
the flick of salt
a whisper of milk

I am a switch of white birch
a stripe of lime
the cackle of bark
a glint of brine

I am a switch of white birch.

Cedar

for Jake

This is the kind of timber that crackles very quietly
as it glows tomato glass, the kind of tinder
that smelts amber on my tongue.

The kind of burning that finds me
even when I'm out on a limb with three kids but no fuel
pulling home to hot pepper broth and kisses of ash.

This is the kind of heat that holds it together
and cinders stray worries to wisp,
the bloom of copper in the night.

Seek, in the belly of this blood bright log
light through flesh,
petals toasting on coals,

the pink surprise of flame, and finding again
in the tap of scarlet scree
the spark that made it all start.

Blue Nails

He wanted bright blue nails, like me.
They made him magic, and he cast spells
conjuring eels and glittering fish.
He is connected to the moon.
When it is large it makes his head large.
He is small when it is small.
It is difficult to sleep when it is full
because of the silver thread that connects them.

He wields his shards of blue
and skips, invisible, down the hill.

Later, he scratched it off because they told him *it's for girls.*
Bright chips littered his school trousers.
I held him. I opened my pot of rose and lemon cream and
he pressed it on his cheeks. But one day
I know some hound will detect it. Tell him *it's for girls.*
I give him pearls to throw and tell him it is fear and
girls and boys are not cut from gingerbread casts.

But I am only one woman and they are many.

One day he comes home beaming.
Between his finger and thumb
is a tiny book, pages small as stamps.
A girl-flower made it for him.
He knows from the silver leaves
that she is his best friend. He shines.

The next day he cannot play
with Daisy because *she is a girl.*

He begins to smile less at the trees
and to pull against the moon.

I bottle magic in the moonlight
and prepare for battle.

Sand

He cries sand again this morning,
freckles rolling down his cheek, beads
of grit he sometimes flicks with his tongue
and crunches, yearning for ice.

His eyes have never been drier,
streaks of silt hatched with crimson
scratches, rubbed shingle with
the back of his sleeve.

It's getting in his ears now
and even in his hair. But we are lucky
today, there's no wind to fan drought
and whip his small face

and we smile about this and I whisper
spring splash and drenched eyelashes
and when he moves away
my ear tickles with beach.

Light Work

I licked blackberry blood from my fingers
as he told me *many hands make life work Mum*

that's what I told them Mum and it worked
he beamed, *it worked, I said what you said*

and they let me join in. I put the berries down.
Many hands make life work? Oh yes, I replied

and we smiled our eyes and we drank our milk
and I left proud stains on his arms.

What Colour is the Wind?

she asked, expecting me to squeeze it onto her plate
so she could get on with painting her box.

I scoured the line for pants and sheets,
for sandstorms and ripped flags, for slanted sleet
and seagulls blown off course.

Then I searched the cupboards for the whisked rough of dirt
and shocked glass, for whipped clouds that hurt
and shake the house when it storms.

Mum? she called. And she waited with her brush.

Sheffield to Aleppo

It's only a firework I whisper
thumb tucked into her palm

but her eyes reflect a spark
that tells me that somewhere

she knows this isn't quite true –
that a shot can echo when stars skim seas
that shrapnel can whistle through waves
screeching fear in bruising skies

and I stroke floss hair and sweet-bun cheeks
damp from steam, breathing milk
and I ache for it *only to be fireworks*

for thumbs in the dark to be enough
to stop glazed buns cracking in the dust
for shells that spill only golden fish
for grazes that heal with the fizz

of a rocket and I kneel
in the night and feel her sleep.

Acknowledgements

I am grateful to the editors of *And Other Poems, Stand, Atrium, Strix, Laldy*, Three Drops Press, *Foxglove Journal* and *Now Then* where some of these poems first appeared.

'Postnatal Ward' was awarded Fourth Prize in the York Literature Poetry Prize 2018; 'Oyster' came Second in the Mother's Milk Books Writing Competition 2017; 'Aubade', 'Fruit', 'Track', 'Slow Ship' and 'Stones' were shortlisted for the 2017 Flambard Poetry Prize; 'Amber' was shortlisted for the *London Magazine* Poetry Prize 2016 and 'Soul Seed' was longlisted for the Plough Prize, 2016.

I am grateful to everyone at Valley Press for believing in this book, especially Jamie McGarry. My thanks also go to the Thursday night poetry group at the University of Leeds, to John Whale, and to everyone in the online 3030 group. Personal thanks are due to Carole Bromley, Malika Booker, Kate Garrett, Rebecca Goss, Char March and Helen Mort for their encouragement, inspiration and advice with editing some of these pieces. Special thanks and love go to my family and friends for their support. And finally, I thank the vibrant poetry community in Sheffield, without which this book would not have been possible.